Family Home Evening

FOR NEWLYWEDS

BY DEBORAH PACE ROWLEY

Family Home Evening for Newlyweds:
© 2002, 2004 Deborah Pace Rowley
All rights reserved.

No portion of this book may be reproduced by any means
without written permission from the publisher,
Aspen Books
290 E. 2020 N. Provo, UT 84604

Printed in the United States of America
Banta Book Group
10 9 8 7 6 5 4 3 2

Book design by Jeanette Andrews

ISBN: 1-56236-250-X

ASPEN
BOOKS

*C*ongratulations on your marriage and welcome to *Family Home Evenings for Newlyweds*! You are the perfect couple for this book. If you have leisure time and a little money or if you have no free time and no money, this book is for you. It doesn't matter if you grew up with F.H.E. or if you have never had a Family Home Evening lesson before. You may want to go all out for family night or you may be thinking, "I'll do this if it doesn't take too much work." The only thing that matters is that you love each other and have a desire to grow closer and stronger as a family. If you are committed to following the prophet's counsel, this book will help you to establish a pattern for Family Home Evening that will last through all the children and challenges that lie in the years ahead.

There are 80 Family Home Evening lessons in this book—more than enough for a year. The first thing you need to do is decide together on a specific time to hold Family Home Evening each week. Monday may work best for your schedules, or Saturday of Sunday may be better. The most important thing is to establish a set time. If you decide you will work Family Home Evening in when you can, it probably won't happen. Most of the lessons can be completed in 1/2 hour, although the amount of time you spend is up to you. The amount of work you do to prepare is also up to you. There are 56 lessons that require no preparation and no money. All you have to do is open the book, turn to a lesson, and follow the instructions. These lessons are found in Section 1 and Section 4. Section 4 contains holiday lessons that need to be scheduled at certain times of the year.

Section 2 contains lessons that require advanced preparation. For these lessons you will need specific items that may cost money if you can't find them around the house. Section 3 contains lessons that you will do away from home, and some of these cost money as well. Pick a lesson out of Section 2 or Section 3 when you want to take more time and do something a little different.

The lessons don't need to be done in any special order. Pick and choose the ones that appeal to you. You can even repeat a favorite lesson. Family Home Evening is usually just for you and your spouse, but occasionally you may want to invite another couple over to share family night with you. Below, there is a list of lessons from all four sections that would work well with two or more couples. Good luck! I hope you will enjoy getting to know each other, communicating about your relationship, growing in the gospel, and having fun. That is what Family Home Evening is all about.

LESSONS TO USE WITH OTHER COUPLES

TABLE OF CONTENTS

SECTION ONE
To be done at home / No cost involved / No Preparation required

SECTION TWO
To be done at home / May cost money / Preparation required

SECTION THREE
To be done outside of the home / May Cost Money

SECTION FOUR

Holidays lessons / To be done at home
No money or preparation needed

SECTION FIVE

Games and Activities

S C A V E N G E R   H U N T

Go on a scavenger hunt at home! Both of you take your own paper sack, and fill it with 10 objects that represent the things listed below. As soon as you have found everything, get back together to show and tell.

1. Yourself
2. Your spouse
3. Dating experiences
4. Engagement
5. Wedding

6. Honeymoon
7. Married life
8. Your home
9. Greatest strength as a couple
10. Your future together

(For example, a clock could represent your engagement because time moved so slowly. A key could be the wedding because it opened a new door in your life.)

ead the following: When you let the love you have for your spouse wither and die, you are apostatizing from your marriage covenant. You have as much responsibility to keep your love alive as you do to keep your testimony of the gospel alive. How do you keep this love alive? One way is to show it! Create a list of the different ways you can show love to each other. Discuss what you have written, then identify the top ten ways to show love. Now cut the list in half, and each of you take half. Commit to use those five ways to show love during the coming week.

Gather several pieces of paper and a pencil and place the Gospel Draw Cards in a paper sack. (Make the cards by cutting the words on pages 85 and 87 apart.) Take turns drawing a card and reading the name on the card. The names are well-known people from the scriptures or church history. Next draw a picture or pictures to help your spouse guess who the person is. No words or numbers are allowed. Keep track of the time it takes to correctly guess each name. The spouse with the shortest time spent drawing wins.

~⚬ T E S T I M O N Y   T I M E ⚬~

*W*rite down your testimony of the gospel of Jesus Christ. How did you gain knowledge of the truthfulness of the gospel? When did you realize you had a testimony? What experiences have you had to strengthen that testimony? Recording how you feel about the Savior, His message, the scriptures, and the prophets will help you realize how important these things are to you. This written testimony will also help your spouse get to know you better. Sharing spiritual experiences will bring you closer as a couple because you are inviting the Spirit of the Lord to share your relationship. After you have written your testimonies, read them to each other. Then keep them in a special place and update them regularly.

SIMILES AND SMILES

Create some similes (comparisons) to describe each other. Write a simile to describe your spouse in each of the categories listed below. Make sure you include reasons for the simile you choose. Next share what you wrote with each other.

1. Car
2. Food
3. Shoe
4. Animal

5. Color
6. Season
7. Cartoon character
8. Sport

9. Place
10. Movie star

(For example, you are like an SUV because you're adventurous and love the great outdoors.)

Complete the sentences by filling in the blanks. When you are finished, share your responses with each other.

1. You make me laugh when _____.

2. You make me love you when _____.

3. You make me happy when _____.

4. You help me feel special when _____.

5. You help me feel closer to Heavenly Father when _____.

6. You make me feel good-looking when _____.

7. You make me feel like becoming better when _____.

8. You make me smile when _____.

9. You cheer me up when _____.

10. You help me feel loved when _____.

11. You strengthen my testimony when _____.

12. You make me proud of you when _____.

*E*ach of you spend a few minutes locating your favorite verse in the scriptures. Then share these verses with each other. As you read them, give reasons why the scripture is so meaningful to you. When you are done, try to memorize the scriptures and write them on cards to hang somewhere in your home.

HEAR ME OUT

*T*his listening exercise will help improve your communication skills. Choose one spouse to go first, and be sure to follow these rules:

- The "talking" spouse talks about himself/herself nonstop for 15 minutes.

- The "listening" spouse doesn't say anything.

- When the 15 minutes is up, the roles are reversed and the "listening" spouse becomes the "talking" spouse and vice versa.

When you aren't talking, listen intently to what your spouse is saying. In this activity, your listening will improve because you won't have to spend listening time trying to think of how to respond.

Write letters of the alphabet down the left hand side of a sheet of paper. Then write a work or phrase to describe your spouse next to each letter. On the letter "A" for example you could write Always Smiling, "B" Beautiful, and so on. Be creative and positive! Use a dictionary if needed. When you're finished, get together and share your alphabet.

Tell each other family history stories that you remember. What stories were you told about your parents when they were children? What do you know about their courtship or conversion? What stories do you remember about your grandparents or great-grandparents? What memorable things have happened in your own life that you want to tell your children? You may want to take notes so that you can pass these stories on to future generations. Spiritual experiences and missionary experiences that strengthen the testimonies of others are important to include in your family history.

*I*magine that you had $2,000 to spend on each other. Make a list of all the things that you would buy your spouse. Estimate the value of the items on the list as you go. When you are finished, exchange lists and dream of winning a sweepstakes someday.

*R*ecall three or four times in your relationship when you felt completely and totally loved. Share these experiences with each other. Describe the experience and how you felt in as much detail as possible, then place each instance in one of the categories below.

People are usually one of three types:

Auditory *(need to be told that they are loved)*

Visual *(need to be shown that they are loved through action, gifts, dates, etc.)*

Kinesthetic *(need to be touched to know they are loved)*

Everyone enjoys all three, but generally one need is dominant. Discuss together which category each of you fall in. When you know which type of people you and your spouse are, you will be able to help each other feel totally loved more often.

BAGS OF BLESSINGS

Set the timer for three minutes and write down as many blessings as you can think of during that time. Write as quickly as you can and put down everything that comes to your mind. When the time is up, compare your lists. What blessings do you have in common? What blessings are different? Combine your lists and add some more blessings to create a master list of "100 Things We are Grateful For." Post your list on the fridge and refer to it often during the week. Next Family Night you may want to discuss how thinking about your blessings and having the list posted affected your attitudes and behavior during the week.

Write love notes for each other. Next have your spouse step outside for a few minutes while you race around the house hiding notes so that your spouse can find them during the week. Be as creative in your hiding places as possible.

Next, you wait outside while your spouse does the same thing. When both of you have hidden your notes, sing all the Primary songs you can remember together. Now enjoy Family Home Evening all week long as notes turn up in unexpected places.

*E*valuate your marriage in each of the areas below. (Rank your responses on a scale of 1 to 10, with 1 being a weak area that you need to focus on immediately, 5 indicating that you are doing okay in that area, and 10 being a strength with no need for improvement.

After you discuss your responses, make a goal to strengthen one of the areas.

1. Common goals and values

2. Commitment to growth

3. Communication skills

4. Creative, productive use of conflict

5. Appreciation and affection

6. Agreement on roles

7. Cooperation and teamwork

8. Sexual fulfillment

9. Money management

10. Spiritual growth

*T*ake one of the word association lists and look at the six words on it. (These lists are on page 89.) Then write down the first thing that comes into your mind as you think about each word. (For example, snow = skiing or winter.)

When you have completed all six words, set a timer for 60 seconds. Read the list of association words to your partner one at a time. Your partner will call out things in an attempt to guess the word that you wrote down. You can't give hints but you can say when he/she gets one right. If one word is taking too long, pass to the next word. Your partner gets a point for every one that he/she gets right in one minute. Next, switch roles with a new list. The spouse with the most points when all the lists have been used wins.

*P*resident Spencer W. Kimball taught, "The marriage that is based upon selfishness is almost certain to fail . . . The one who marries to give happiness as well as receive it, to give service as well as to receive it, and looks after the interests of the two and then the family as it comes will have a good chance that the marriage will be a happy one" (***Marriage*** Salt Lake City: Deseret Book, 1981, p.44).

This activity will help you avoid selfishness by focusing on your partner's needs instead of your own.

It is easy in marriage to concentrate on what your spouse isn't doing for you, but much harder to recognize your own failures. This activity will help you focus on your partner's needs instead of your own.

First, write down five needs you feel your spouse has. (For example: The need to feel attractive, the need to have my support in his church calling, etc)

Next, write what you are doing to meet those needs right now. Chose one area where you feel you could be doing more. Identify several specific things you can do to meet this need. You can share these lists with each other, or you can simply work on them privately the rest of the week.

Read your patriarchal blessings to each other. Then read and discuss this statement: "Never ask the question, did I marry the right one? Once you have been sealed, you have married the perfect one—not because that person is perfect but because you yourself are determined to be the perfect companion. Your spouse will be as perfect as you are or as perfect as you allow him/her to be and encourage him/her to be."

Finally answer this question: How can we help each other achieve the promises in our patriarchal blessings?

Work together to design your dream house. You can write about it or draw it. Include a floor plan and description of each room. Talk about everything you will need to make your dream home complete. Remember that your house is an extension of your personality. What does your home say about the two of you?

~ TRADITION ~

*D*iscuss the following questions:

1. What are the things you remember best about your childhood?

2. What traditions do you remember around the holidays?

3. What gospel-related traditions did your family have?

4. What do you remember about Family Home Evening?

5. What are some traditions you want to continue or start with your own family?

DIGGING DEEP

*P*lace the Digging Deep Cards upside down between you. (Make the cards by cutting apart the questions on pages 91–101.) Take turns drawing a card and answering the question. As soon as you have responded, you can ask your spouse to comment on the same question or pick up a new card. If you don't have an answer for a question, draw a different card and continue on.

*L*ook up these scriptures, find the words, and write them down. You can do this together or as a race.

Alma 55:24 . . . . .4th line, 4th word

Alma 5:57 . . . . .4th line, 8th word

Mosiah 2:9 . . . . .14th line, 3rd word

3 Nephi 17:23 . . . . . . .3rd line, 1st word

Mosiah 2:9 . . . . .10th line, 6th word

3 Nephi 17:2 . . . . . . .2nd line, 4th word

3 Nephi 4:33 . . . . .1st line, 3rd word

Now unscramble the words to create a phrase, then discuss the phrase. How do you accomplish what the phrase says? You may wish to read King Benjamin's words beginning with Mosiah 2:9. Mosiah 4 is loaded with wisdom.

*W*rite a goal statement to guide your relationship as a couple. Generally, this statement consists of three to five things you want to accomplish together as a couple (For example: We will include the Lord as a partner in our marriage through daily prayer, scripture reading, etc.)

Focus on spiritual, emotional, mental, physical, social, or financial areas. Try to get down to what you feel is absolutely essential for you to achieve happiness and success in this life. Phrase your statements positively as things you will do, rather than things you hope to do or will try to do. Refer to these goals often.

❦ K I D   Q U I Z ❧

Answer the following questions:

1. How many kids do you want?

2. What children's names do you like?

3. How many boys and how many girls would you like?

4. How will you discipline your children?

5. What do you think is the most important thing parents can give their children?

6. What do you think will be the best thing about being a parent?

7. What do you think will be the hardest thing about being a parent?

8. What makes a good mom?

9. What makes a good dad?

10. What do you hope your kids will say about you as a parent?

*C*omplete two family trees, one for both your families. (The family trees are found on pages 103 and 104.) If possible, call your parents for any information you don't know. When the family trees are complete, put them in a Family Treasures Box. (Any sturdy box will do.)

Add to the box old family photos and any items that have been passed on to you from your parents, grandparents, or great-grand parents (letters, histories, keepsakes, etc.). Make sure you include special things that belonged to you and your parents. Give a description of each item, including who it belonged to and why it is significant.

Each of you make a list of the five best days you have experienced in your life so far. What days stand out as being the most memorable or important or happiest? If you can, number them from 1 to 5 with 1 being the greatest day.

When you have finished with your lists, share them with each other. Describe the days that you have written down. Why were they so significant? What days can you picture in your future together that you think will make it into the top ten.

❧ H A P P Y   F A C E ❧

*M*arriage can sometimes be a roller-coaster ride of emotions. It's easy to start thinking you have no control over how you feel or that your spouse controls your moods. This activity helps you understand your feelings a little better.

Answer the following questions:

1. What are you doing when you feel the happiest?

2. What situations often trigger feelings of discouragement or depression?

3. What things work in lifting your spirits when you are down?

4. What can you do to be happy more often?

5. What can your partner do to assist you in choosing to be happy?

6. What can your partner do to help you change you mood when you are upset or depressed? (And what shouldn't they do!)

≈ L I F E   I N V E N T O R Y ≈

$\mathcal{C}$omplete the following life inventory questions.

1. What things make me feel that life is really worth living? When do I feel fully alive?

2. What do I do well? What do I have to contribute to the lives of others?

3. What dreams do I have for the future? What goals do I want to start working on?

4. What qualities do I need to develop to fulfill my dreams? What resources do I have to assist me in accomplishing my goals?

5. What attitudes do I need to change? What weaknesses do I need to strengthen so that I can accomplish these things?

6. What should I start doing now?

Follow through on question #6 by reporting how you are doing next week in Family Home Evening. Your spouse is your greatest coach, cheering section, and fan club. Make sure you take advantage of this wonderful tool.

Often people have unrealistic expectations of marriage that end up creating conflict. Read the list below. Some experts suggest that these are dangerous myths of marriage that cause problems for couples that cling to them.

Do you believe any of these statements? See if you and you spouse can turn each statement around so that it reflects the truth about marriage.

1. Marriage should always make you happier than when you were single.

2. The romance will stay alive if you really love each other.

3. Your mate should automatically understand you

4. In a good marriage, partners have identical dreams and goals.

5. If your sex life starts out good, it will stay that way.

6. If you have to work at marriage, something is wrong.

7. You should work on changing your spouse for the better.

8. Happily married couples should never fight

9. You can't find self-fulfillment in marriage or family relationships.

10. Your ideas about an ideal marriage should not change.

WOMAN OF THE YEAR

The husband should give this lesson to honor his wife. Imagine that she has just won the "Woman of the Year" award. Give a speech of tribute to her and an imaginary audience stating why you feel she has won the award and why you appreciate her influence in your life.

~C L A S S I C   C O U P L E S~

*O*ut the Couples Cards in a paper sack. (Make the cards by cutting apart the names of couples found on page 107. Try not to look at the names as you cut them!) On each card are the names of a famous duo.

Take turns drawing a card and trying to get your spouse to guess what names are on the card. You can use gestures, and you can also say words that the couple might say as long as you don't use their names or the name of the movie, book, play, etc., that they are associated with. (For example: Romeo might say, "I love you even though my family hates you.")

Here is a hint: The couples come from history, the scriptures, movies, TV, literature, or current events.

NEWLYWED NOTES

See how well you know each other! Gather several pieces of paper and pencils, then place the Newlywed Cards upside down between you. (Make the cards by cutting apart the statements on pages 109 and 111.)

Take turns drawing a card and reading the phrase on the back. If your spouse draws the card and reads, "Favorite Color," he/she writes down a guess at your favorite color. You write down the correct answer, then compare answers. If the answers match, your spouse gets one point. Now it's your turn to draw a card and answer a question about your spouse. The one with the most points at the end of the game wins!

INTO THE FUTURE

 *W*rite predictions about your life in 5 years, 10 years, and 25 years. Predict what you will be doing, where you will be living, how many children you will have, and what things you will have accomplished. Be as specific as possible. You can work on making these predictions together or write them individually and compare notes.

L O V E   I S   .   .   .

Read the definitions of love below. Then write 20 definitions of your own. What is love to the two of you? When you are finished, post your list where you can see it.

Love is sharing the hard times.

Love is laughing at the same old joke.

Love is having a cold and your spouse still kisses you.

Love is walking hand and hand in the moonlight.

Love is forgiving your spouse even though he/she makes you furious.

Love is being swept off your feet.

Love is the greatest thing in the world.

Research together the topic of having your calling and election made sure. What does this mean? As you look up scriptures and discuss this topic, keep a record in a notebook or journal of what you discover. What does receiving the Second Comforter have to do with this? Use the topical guide to get you started. You can also use Priesthood or Relief Society manuals or books by apostles to help you in your search. How can the two of you work toward this goal together?

HUSBAND OF THE YEAR

This lesson should be given by the wife to honor her husband. Imagine that your husband has been nominated for the prestigious "Husband of the Year" award. In order to win, you need to give a speech to convince the judges that your husband is the greatest husband around. Talk about the qualities that your husband has that you appreciate. You might want to express your gratitude for the priesthood that he holds and tell him why it is so important to you that he honors his priesthood as he does.

❧ S T R E S S   T E S T ❧

*L*ife can be stressful. This test will help you see how you deal with stress. Answer each question with a number from 1 to 5. (1 if the answer is "no," and 5 if the answer is "absolutely yes.")

1. Do you tire easily, lack energy and feel fatigued often?

2. Do you feel like you work hard but get nothing accomplished?

3. Do you find yourself being negative and critical more often than you would like?

4. Are you invaded by a feeling of sadness that you can't explain?

5. Are you forgetting things such as deadlines and appointments?

6. Are you spending less time with your family and close friends?

7. Are you more irritable and more easily upset?

8. Does joy seem elusive and impossible to obtain?

9. Do you get sick often? (Aches, pains, headaches, colds you can't get rid of)

10. Do you dread getting up in the morning or dread the end of the weekend?

Add up the numbers from all your answers. 0-15 you are doing fine; 16-35 you need to make a few changes; 36-50 you have a high level of stress and need to make some major changes. Determine what you can do to eliminate or more effectively handle some of the factors causing you stress.

For this activity you are going to write some acrostic poems together. An acrostic poem is made up of descriptive words or phrased that begin with each letter of a person's name. (For example: For a person named Amy, the poem may be: A= Athletic; M= Magical Dancer; Y= Young and energetic.)

Create an acrostic poem for both of you, using your first and last names; you can even use your middle name if you like. The lines can describe your appearance, personality, actions, abilities, talents, or whatever. Let the poet in you go wild.

*M*arriages can be strengthened when you share a secret language all your own. It is fun to be able to communicate secretly with each other even when people surround you. Think of two or three phrases that you might want to say to each other without anyone else knowing. (For example, I love you, You look gorgeous, Let's get out of here, etc.)

Next, think of some gestures that you could use to communicate those phrases. Signals are only one way to express your love. Some couples use nicknames or code words to say, "I love you." Think about the unique ways that you show your love. Adding to this list increases both the love you have and the ways you can express it.

FAMILY PRIDE

*C*ountries, states, and even cities do many things to create pride in the people who live there. Family pride can be created in the same way. First, choose a popular song or hymn that expresses your feelings about your family or describes the things that are most important to your family.

Next, choose a bird, animal, or flower to represent you and explain the reason you chose this symbol. Write a motto that expresses your philosophy of life and the attitude you have about the world. Choose a family scripture. This scripture should be a favorite scripture or a scripture that will guide and direct you as a family. Finally, design a family crest or flag including some, if not all, of the things listed above. Hang them up or save them to build and strengthen family pride in your children in the future.

*G*rab some paper and go to separate places to write. Think about all the reasons you love your in-laws. Write 10 positive things about your spouse's parents and then 10 positive things about his/her brothers and sisters. When you have completed your lists, get back together to share what you have written.

Remember to focus on the positive. Family Home Evening is not the time to bring up complaints or tease each other about the things your families do that bug you. Learning to love your in-laws will only strengthen and deepen your love for each other.

T P   T R A I L S

Take the roll of toilet paper off the holder in the bathroom, then sit on the floor. Start by taking the roll and beginning to unroll it. While you are unrolling, complete this statement: "I am glad to be married to you because…" You can't stop listing the reasons until the tissue is completely unrolled! The more toilet paper on the roll, the more reasons you need to come up with.

When you are finished, hand the empty tube to your spouse. He/she will then roll the toilet paper back on to the roll while giving reasons why he/she is glad to be married to you. After this lesson you can put the lumpy roll back in the bathroom, and all week you will remember the things that were said.

Spend a few minutes creating a list of five people who have significantly influenced your life for good. Think of people you look up to and admire, people who were there at critical moments in your life. When you have finished this list, make another list of the ways your spouse influences you for good. When you have completed both lists, share them with each other. Then discuss how you would like to be an influence for good in other people's lives.

HAND IN HAND

When you were engaged, people probably thought that you had been surgically joined at the hip! Now you can re-create that unity by spending an entire evening hand in hand.

You will need to begin this lesson before dinner. Take a bandanna or scarf and tie your left hand to your partner's right hand at the wrist. Now go about making dinner as you normally would except for the fact that you have an extra appendage and only one free hand! Eat dinner and clean up, then do some laundry, iron some clothes, or water the lawn. You choose the activity as long as you do it attached to each other. This is great for learning teamwork and cooperation. (Eating spaghetti for dinner is particularly entertaining! Don't untie your hands until the evening is over or until you feel like a missionary, whichever comes first.

⚜ C A L E N D A R   C R E A T I O N ⚜

Take a yearly calendar or make a calendar of your own. Go through the year month by month listing important dates. Include the birthdays of all your extended family, including parents, brothers, sisters, etc. Note significant anniversaries (at least your own!). Jot down holidays you want to remember such as Mother's Day. Then plan some mini-celebrations for the two of you.

Some people celebrate the day of their first date every year, when they first met, when they kissed for the first time, or when he proposed. Most people celebrate their anniversary, but in strong marriages, couples celebrate their relationship continually. Post this calendar somewhere visible, then when "your" holidays approach, celebrate with a card or a small gift or a special activity.

❧ T H I S   I S   M Y   L I F E ❧

Set aside one hour for this Family Home Evening. During this hour, you are going to start and finish your life history. Begin with your name. Then give the place, date, and time of your birth. Write the name of the doctor and the hospital. Tell briefly about your family. List the names of each family member in order.

Describe your childhood briefly. Focus mainly on the places you lived and the schools you attended. List important church callings, mission, endowment dates, etc. Write the date and the location of your marriage and the full name of your spouse. List the jobs that you have held and tell about your career. End by listing any special recognition, accomplishments, talents, awards etc.

That is it! You have your life history written. Later you can give information about your children and add more specific details.

For this Family Home Evening you will be sharing some of the spiritual experiences that you have had with each other. Listed below are several categories. The first category is prayer. If you have had a spiritual experience related to prayer and you feel comfortable talking about it, share it with your partner. You may not have had an experience to share in every area, and some experiences that you have had will not fit in any of the areas that are listed. The list is simply a guide to help you get started sharing some of the most precious and meaningful experiences of your life.

1. Prayer
2. Priesthood
3. Testimony
4. Service
5. Temples

6. Missionary work
7. Scripture study
8. Tithing
9. Blessings
10. Miracles

11. Feeling the Spirit
12. Callings
13. Revelation
14. Prophets and apostles
15. Jesus Christ

MONEY MATTERS

Finances can cause big problems in a relationship. Arguments over money are more frequent in most marriages than fights over anything else. This is the case even though money and material things are completely insignificant in the eternal scheme of things.

Many prophets have outlined basic principles to follow for prosperity and success. Read the list of principles below then discuss how you are doing in each of the areas. Be especially careful to avoid blame if you are falling short in any area. Work together to determine how you can improve.

1. Pay an honest tithing first.

2. Pay a generous fast offering.

3. Live on less than you earn.

4. Learn to tell the difference between your needs and wants.

5. Develop and live within a budget.

6. Pay yourself each month by adding even a little bit to your savings.

❧ S N A P S H O T ❧

*F*ind a photograph or a snapshot from your wedding that is a duplicate or that you don't want to save. Cut it between the bride and the groom like two puzzle pieces, then each of you write a thank you note on the back of the puzzle piece with you on it.

Express your appreciation to one set of parents for everything they did to help make the big day so wonderful. When you are done, send the two pieces in two separate envelopes. Be sure to include a note in one of the envelopes that says, "We couldn't have come together without you."

You might want to photocopy the photo first, then you'll have two matching photos and you can thank both sets of your parents.

KISS LIST

For this activity you will need a bag of Hershey's kisses. Cut up a piece of paper into thin strips (approximately ½-inch wide and 3 inches long). Then separate the strips so that each of you has 10. Write this sentence on each strip, completing it differently every time: I love you because…

Each of you unwrap Hershey's kisses. Try to keep the wrapper as complete as possible. Replace the Hershey's slip with your own slip of paper, and rewrap the kiss. Now you both can open three or four kisses for Family Home Evening, and then open one kiss every day for the following week.

Hold the Spouse Olympics by competing in traditionally male or female events.

Husband Events:

Sewing on a button

Ironing a shirt

Hardboiling an egg

Mopping the floor

Applying make-up

Wife Events:

Pounding nails

Taking out the trash

Tying a tie

Checking the oil

Shining a pair of shoes

Use only the events you have supplies for or substitute some of your own. The person who completes all the events on the list first wins.

*M*ake scripture cookies by looking up the verses and figuring out the ingredients.

Beat together:
    ⅓ cup Psalms 55:21
    1 ½ cups Jeremiah 6:20
    2 Isaiah 10:14

Add:
    2 cups 1 Kings 4:22
    1 teaspoon Song of Solomon 4:14
    1 teaspoon D&C 101:39
    ½ teaspoon 1 Corinthians 4:6
    3 cups D&C 89:17
    1 cup 1 Samuel 30:12

Drop by spoonful onto greased cookie sheet. Bake at 350 degrees for 15 minutes, but not before reading Joseph Smith History 1:37 and D&C 133:11.

Key: Beat together butter or shortening, milk, sugar (1 cup brown, ½ cup white), eggs. Add flour, cinnamon, salt, soda (to make them "puffed up"), oats, and raisins.

*B*ake a batch of cookies to take anonymously to a neighbor or friend. Include with the cookies a note of appreciation written in a secret code.

For example: DV OLEV BLF

Here is the code key: A=Z B=Y C=X D=W E=V and so on.

Include the code key underneath all the cookies or taped to the bottom of the plate.

Now deliver them and run!

*P*ut together a time capsule to be opened in 10 years. Think about the kinds of things your future children will want to see when they help you open the box.

Here are some suggestions:

Pictures of the two of you as you are now

A description of your apartment or house

A tape of your favorite music

Pictures that show popular fashions

Prices of different items

A list of phrases or slang words used now

A newspaper or anything that tells about life today

Finally, place a letter in the capsule from both of you addressed to your future kids. Wrap the box up in wrapping paper. Write on it the date you want it opened and put it somewhere you won't forget.

CAMPOUT

Camp out in your backyard or in the living room. You don't have to travel far to feel like you are getting away. Roll out your spacious sleeping bags, cuddle, and count the stars. Then roast marshmallows over a barbecue grill or your stove. Make S'mores with graham crackers and chocolate chips. The best part is that you can crawl back in your own bed later for a good night's sleep.

MEMORIES ON TAPE

Sit down together and reminisce while a cassette tape is recording your conversation. Talk about your memories of the first time you met, experiences you had while dating, and how you got engaged. Describe your engagement and the wedding, your honeymoon, and the first months of marriage. This could count as another lesson if you listen to this tape in six months or a year. You also might want to include this tape in your time capsule. (See page 56.)

～✲ COLLAGE CREATION ✲～

*D*esign a collage of a successful marriage. Take a large piece of posterboard and attach to it items that illustrate the love you have for each other. Include pictures, cards, ticket stubs, scribbled love notes, a dried rose, or other small things you have given to each other. Arrange them creatively then attach them with tape. This will allow you to change your collage and add to it. Now hang it somewhere in your home. Seeing this visual reminder of your loving, strong marriage will help keep it that way.

C R E P E C O O K I N G

*T*ry cooking crepes together. You need:

3 eggs   3 tablespoons butter, melted
½ cup milk   ½ cup flour
½ cup water   ½ teaspoon salt

Combine all ingredients in a blender, and blend about one minute. Scrape down the sides with a rubber spatula and blend 30 seconds more. To cook, heat omelet, crepe, or regular frying pan on medium-high heat just hot enough to sizzle a drop of water. Brush lightly with a little bit of butter. Pour in just enough batter to cover the bottom of the pan, tipping and tilting the pan to move the batter around. Cook till light brown on the bottom and dry on top. This recipe makes about eight crepes. See which one of you can find the most delicious filling. Try jam, ice cream, chocolate topping, fresh fruit, whipped cream, ham, cheese, vegetables, even scrambled eggs.

❧ PROGRESSION ❧

*H*ave a progressive dinner without leaving home. Begin with an appetizer of fresh fruit or cheese and crackers in the backyard. Then come inside for a salad in the living room. Try sitting on pillows and eating with chopsticks. Move on to the main dish in the dining room or kitchen with candles on the table. Then eat dessert while lounging in bed, and have after-dinner mints in a bubble bath.

reate a candy bar letter for your bishop. Plan what you want to say by using the names of candy bars in your phrases. (For example, "Dear Bishop, you are a 'Life saver.' You are worth '$100,000' to this ward. If we searched the whole 'Milky Way,' we wouldn't find a better bishop than you, etc."

Buy the posterboard and candy bars that you need. Write your letter, leaving space so you can tape the candy bars in the right places. You can sign the letter or have it be from secret admirers. Then deliver it to the bishop to finish up your Family Home Evening.

HUSBAND'S CHOICE

The husband gets to choose an activity for this Family Home Evening. The wife can't complain even if the chosen activity is watching a football game on TV or playing two-on-two basketball. Choose something that doesn't cost money. Go hiking or mountain biking. You could even go to a hardware store and show your wife all the tools you hope to have someday!

WIFE'S CHOICE

The wife gets to choose an activity for this Family Home Evening. The husband can't complain even if the chosen activity is going to a free piano concert or visiting an art gallery. Choose something that doesn't cost money. Go to a craft boutique or walk around a furniture store. Give your husband a taste of the things that you enjoy.

MY NEIGHBORHOOD

Go on a walk around your neighborhood. Take a loaded camera with you, and take pictures as you go. What do you think you will remember about your first neighborhood after you have moved away? Are there people you will never forget? What events have occurred in this neighborhood that you'll remember? If you were to return in your car 10 or 20 years from now, what do you think you would see? When you return home, take a walk around your house or apartment. What will you remember about the first place you lived together? What physical things will stand out (peeling paint in the bathroom, the bright orange carpet in the living room)? If the walls could talk, what would they say? What memories do you have of each room?

To be done outside of the home
May cost money

❧ TEMPLE TRIP ❧

Attend an endowment session in the temple together. While you are in the temple consider these questions:

1. What does the temple teach me about marriage and the relationship between a husband and a wife?

2. What does the temple teach me about being a parent?

After the session, sit in the celestial room and discuss what you learned.

RESTAURANT HOPPING

This is a variation of a progressive dinner but instead of moving from house to house, move from one restaurant to another. The goal is to go to four or five different places without spending more than $10-$15. Go to one place for a drink or hors d'oeuvres, somewhere else for a small salad or soup, another place for the main dish, and another for fruit or dessert to finish off the meal. Have one thing at each place, then move on. You can get food at a fast food restaurant, a deli, or even a supermarket or convenience store.

FIELD TRIP

Get in the car and take a field trip. The goal is to drive down memory lane. This could involve going back to places where you went on dates or places that were important to you when you were engaged. You could go even further back in time and visit your childhood. Go to your old schools, playgrounds, and the home where you grew up. Visit your high school hangouts and the places you worked and played as a teenager. If you have moved away from all of these places, get out photo albums and share what you remember.

SHOPPING SPREE

Go to a nearby store that has a wide variety of inexpensive items. Then separate and roam the aisles until you find the perfect gift for your spouse that costs less than one dollar. Be creative! Once you have bought your gift, keep it a secret until you get home. Then exchange gifts and explain why you chose what you did.

JAILBIRDS

Go toilet papering like you did when you were kids! Choose someone in your ward who you feel needs a cheerful note and some TP! Write the following on a piece of paper in big bright letters or compose a message of you own: We regret to inform you that you have been caught in the act of being terrific. You are hereby sentenced to a great day.

Sneak out after dark with the note, some tape, and a roll of toilet paper or crepe paper. Tiptoe up to the person's door. (Choose someone who doesn't own a ferocious dog.) Tape the note directly to the door at eye level, then tape the toilet paper or crepe paper in strips to the top and bottom of the door frame to create the effect of a jail. Do not tape the toilet paper directly to the door. You want them to open the door in the morning and look out through your toilet paper bars. Wear dark clothing, be careful not to get caught, and have the getaway car ready to go!

TOURIST ON BOARD

Go to the tourist information center where you live and find local attractions you could visit for free. Check into museums, scenic spots, or historic homes or buildings. Then visit one of these places for Family Home Evening. You will be amazed at how many inviting places are in your own backyard.

Go to the library and read children's books to each other. The picture books by Chris VanAllsburg are wonderful and a great place to start. Find the Dr Seuss books you loved as a kid. Reread *Where the Wild Things Are, The Velveteen Rabbit*, or other favorites.

When you have finished exploring the kids' section, recommend adult or adolescent books to each other. Is there anything you read as a teenager or more recently that you loved and want your spouse to read? Check out these books or some books on marriage to read at home.

*G*o on a hunt around town to embarrass each other and have fun. The goal is to speil out your names using letters found in signs and on buildings. (For example, if your husband's name is Kris, you would first drive to K-Mart, jump out of the car, touch the "K," then jump back in the car and race off, hopefully before someone sees you. Then look for an "R" and so on.)

You can't just point to a letter from the car. If you can't actually touch the letter, get as close to it as you can. And you can't touch more than one letter in one sign. Guess how long it is going to take you to do both your names before you start, and try to stay within that time.

FORBIDDEN PLEASURE

Go to a drive-in movie. Pop your own popcorn, and bring your own seat. Go early enough so you can park down close and sit on beanbags or lawn chairs in front of your car. When the movie is over, go to a scenic spot and park! Kissing is allowed!

PHOTO SHOOT

Go to a store that has an automatic photo booth. Generally, these cost $1-$2 for four different photos. Bring funny hats, sunglasses, and masks with you. then see if you can take these things off while the camera is snapping pictures of the two of you. Use your best funny faces for some hysterical pictures you can keep in your wallet for years to come.

SECTION FOUR
*Holiday lessons / To be done at home
No money or preparation required*

NEW YEAR'S

To celebrate New Year's, write some Anti-Resolutions together. Instead of coming up with a long list of things you should do, this year come up with a few things you are not going to do (For example: I resolve not to leave my socks on the floor. I resolve not to hog the covers. I resolve not to turn the laundry pink anymore.)

Post your list of Anti-Resolutions where you can see them often so that you can remember not to do these things. Don't worry about all the things you could—and maybe should—be doing. Just focus on getting rid of something. It's easier.

VALENTINE'S DAY

To celebrate Valentine's Day, write persuasive valentines to each other. Begin with this phrase: Be mine because...." Then include all the reasons you can think of why your spouse would want to be yours forever. Why would you make a great valentine? Sell yourself! It might be harder to convince your spouse than you think.

To celebrate Easter, make a list of 20 attributes of Christ. For each attribute find a scripture that describes that quality or relates of an experience that illustrates that characteristic in the Savior. These attributes can be adjectives such as loving, patient, and thankful or nouns such as friend, teacher, and son. Pick one of these attributed that you want to develop in your own life to help you become more like Jesus Christ.

HALLOWEEN

To celebrate Halloween, create inexpensive costumes together with supplies you have at home. A robe, some slippers, a green facial mask and hair rollers can transform any beautiful girl into a haggard housewife. Some baggy pants, a stuffed pillow and a growth of beard painted on with mascara can transform any guy into a lazy couch potato husband. Be sure to take lots of pictures when you are done. Then send the photos to friends with this caption, "Here is what a few months of marriage will do to you!"

THANKSGIVING

To celebrate Thanksgiving, count your many blessings. Create a list of the top ten things you are most grateful for. As you share your lists, explain why you are thankful for each thing that you included.

CHRISTMAS

To celebrate Christmas, give a gift to the Savior. At the beginning of December, write down a gift you want to give Christ. This should be a goal to become more like Him in some area of your life. (For example, you could commit to read the scriptures more consistently.)

When you have written down your goal, place it in a box, wrap it up, and put it under the tree. Work on this gift the month of December, then on Christmas Day, open this gift and think about how well you did in accomplishing your goal.

✣ ANNIVERSARY ✣

To help celebrate your anniversary, write love letters to each other. You don't need to quote poetry, just express how you feel after one complete year of marriage. These questions might help you get started:

What do you love most about your spouse?

What are the highlights of the past year?

What are you looking forward to in the future?

How has your love changed or grown?

SECTION FIVE
Games and Activities

Cards and worksheets that go with specific lessons

GOSPEL DRAW CARDS
(To be used with Gospel Draw Lesson on page 3)

King Benjamin	The Three Nephites	Alma the Younger
Lehi	2,000 Stripling Warriors	Esther
Nephi	Helaman	Ruth
Samuel the Lamanite	Ammon	Moroni
Laban	Enos	Mormon

Abraham	Peter, James, and John	Emma Smith
Isaac	Sampson	Solomon
Adam	Mary	Abinadi
Eve	John the Baptist	Daniel
Elijah	Jacob and Esau	Lazarus
Moses	Joseph Smith	Pontius Pilate
Noah	Brigham Young	Paul

WORD ASSOCIATION LISTS

(To be used with Mind Games Lesson on page 16)

List 1
Autumn
Restaurant
Occupation
Marriage
Exercise
Olympics

List 2
Winter
Vacation
Television
Tree
Old
Baby

List 3
Summer
President
Flower
Star
Sport
Country

List 4
Teacher
Prophet
Computer
Clouds
Garden
Jail

List 5
Father
Football
Fire
Hawaii
Test
Car

List 6
Spring
Moon
Holiday
Movie
Nature
Santa Claus

List 7
Ice Cream
Train
Doll
Mother
Church
Mexico

List 8
Love
Shark
Present
Motorcycle
America
Sleep

List 9
Russia
Emotion
High School
Police
Book
Airplane

List 10
Animal
Pizza
Flag
Anger
Money
Drug

List 11
Bear
Grand Canyon
Ring
Grass
Refrigerator
Kiss

List 12
Fingernails
Dog
Tuxedo
Rich
Ocean
Dream

List 13
Hollywood
Disney
Dance
Fruit
Artist
Basketball Team

List 14
Cartoon
Store
Mountain
Hospital
Rain
Nurse

List 15
Circus
Space
Senses
Spy
Telephone
France

How are you like your brothers and sisters?	What quality do you admire most in other people?	What is one thing that scares you?
Who is your favorite relative and why?	What is the one thing you want to do before you die?	What do you like best about the place you live?
What is your favorite time of day and why?	How do you feel about death?	What is one nightmare you remember?

(To be used with Digging Deep Lesson on page 21)

Who is your greatest role model?	What is your favorite way to relax?	If you could travel back in time, where would you want to end up?
What is one thing you have done that you regret?	If you could experience one moment in your life again, which one would you choose?	What is your saddest childhood memory?
If you could travel anywhere, where would you go?	What is your most embarrassing moment?	If you could change one thing about the world, what would it be?

(To be used with Digging Deep Lesson on page 21)

What is your best memory of your teenage years?	What is your greatest accomplishment?	If you were stranded on a desert island, what three things would you want with you?
What is your worst memory of your teenage years?	What is the best time to get up in the morning?	If you had a million dollars, what would you spend it on?
What is your biggest dream?	What is the best time to go to bed at night?	If you could trade places with someone for a day, who would it be?

(To be used with Digging Deep Lesson on page 21)

If you had three wishes, what would they be?	How high is your self-esteem?	What is your favorite hymn?
If you could be any animal, what kind of animal would you be?	What would you like to be remembered for?	What causes you the most stress?
If you could change one thing about yourself, what would it be?	What do you admire most about your parents?	What is your ideal church calling?

(To be used with Digging Deep Lesson on page 21)

Who was your most influential teacher?	What is your dominant emotion?	What excites you?
What do you wish you had time for?	What concerns you most about our country?	How are you different from your siblings?
What do you like best about yourself?	What is your biggest weakness?	How are you different from your parents?

(To be used with Digging Deep Lesson on page 21)

What do you wish you knew more about?	What talents do you have?	What does God think of you?
What do you have to offer the world?	What is a talent you feel you should develop?	What spiritual gifts have you been blessed with?
What do you think your divine mission is?	What do others think of you?	

Great Grandfather

Great Grandfather

Great Grandfather

Great Grandfather

Great Grandmother

Great Grandmother

Great Grandmother

Great Grandmother

Grandfather

Grandmother

Grandfather

Grandmother

Father

Mother

My Family Tree

Me

Great Grandfather

Great Grandmother

Grandfather

Great Grandfather

Great Grandmother

Grandmother

Great Grandfather

Great Grandmother

Grandfather

Great Grandfather

Great Grandmother

Grandmother

Father

Mother

My Family Tree

Me

(To be used with Classic Couples Lesson on page 31)

Romeo & Juliet	Ariel & Eric	Beauty & the Beast	Franklin & Eleanor Roosevelt
Anthony & Cleopatra	JFK & Jackie	Aladdin & Jasmine	Rhett Butler & Scarlet O'Hara
Sampson & Delilah	Sonny & Cher	Mork & Mindy	
Adam & Eve	Lehi & Sariah	George & Jane Jetson	Cosette & Marius (*Les Miserables*)
King Arthur & Guinevere	George & Barbara Bush	George & Martha Washington	Mickey & Minnie Mouse
Bonnie & Clyde	Donny & Marie	Mike & Carol Brady	Charlie Brown & the Little Red-Headed Girl
Joseph & Emma Smith	Ronald & Nancy Reagan	Fred Astaire & Ginger Rogers	
Joseph & Mary	Jacob & Rachel (The Old Testament)	Lucy & Ricky (I Love Lucy)	Christine & the Phantom (*Phantom of the Opera*)
Abraham & Sarah	Robin Hood & Maid Marian	Fred & Wilma Flintstone	
Bill & Hillary Clinton	Prince Charles & Diana	Superman & Lois Lane	

Favorite Color	Someone He/She Wants to Meet	Favorite Store
Favorite Food	Biggest Pet Peeve	Greatest Talent
Favorite Book	Favorite Restaurant	Favorite Time of Day
Favorite Movie	Favorite Type of Car	Favorite Season
Favorite Song	Favorite Perfume/Cologne	Favorite Holiday
Favorite Scripture Story	Biggest Fear	Favorite Possession

Best Physical Quality	Favorite Candy	Favorite TV Show
Place He/She Wants to Live	Favorite Cereal	Place He/She Wants to Visit
Favorite Place to Be	Closest Family Member	Favorite Vacation Spot
Favorite Thing to Do	Biggest Dream	Biggest Hero
Favorite Temple	Favorite Movie Star	Least Favorite Household Chore
Favorite Ice Cream Flavor	Favorite Musician or Group	Best Character Trait